THE
IROQUOIS

by Barbara A. McCall

Illustrated by Luciano Lazzarino

ROURKE PUBLICATIONS, INC.

VERO BEACH, FLORIDA 32964

CONTENTS

© 1989 by Rourke Publications, Inc.

Library of Congress Cataloging-in-Publication Data

McCall, Barbara A., 1936-
  The Iroquois / by Barbara A. McCall.
    p.   cm. —(Native American people)
  Includes index.
  Summary: Examines the history, traditional lifestyle, and current situation of the Iroquois Indians.
    1. Iroquois Indians—Juvenile literature. [1. Iroquois Indians. 2. Indians of North America.] I. Title. II. Series.
  E99.I7M43 1989   970.004'97—dc19   88-18188
  ISBN 0-86625-378-5   AC

INTRODUCTION

Millions of years ago, great glaciers covered much of the northern parts of the world. At that time, a land bridge probably connected the continents of Asia and North America. Groups of people migrated from ice-covered Asia across this bridge to the Americas. Slowly they moved south and east in search of land where the hunting was good.

In 1492 Christopher Columbus discovered the descendants of these migrating groups when he reached America. He called the people Indians because he thought he had reached India. Today we honor the Indians as the Native Americans.

For centuries Indians were called "red men," but that was never a correct term. The skin tones of Indians vary from light ivory to a coppery tan. Our Native Americans are members of the Mongoloid race, which makes them relatives of the peoples of China and Japan.

Many Indians welcomed the white traders and settlers to their lands. But soon the whites wanted to possess the land and drive off the Native Americans. Indians believed that the land belonged to a whole tribe. It was theirs to care for, not to own or sell. This was different from the beliefs of the white Europeans who wanted their own parcels of land in the New World.

When the whites first met the Iroquois, the Indians were a powerful force. They controlled the lands that extended from what is now Montreal, Canada, through New York State, and into Pennsylvania. The Iroquois were a highly organized group of five tribes who had great political wisdom. They created a confederacy — called the League of the Iroquois — that was the first form of democracy in the New World. In fact, their confederacy was very much admired by Benjamin Franklin. He encouraged our founding fathers to model parts of our government after the League.

But the great Iroquois Nation quickly lost power after the American Revolution. Their lands were claimed by the new government of the United States, and the Indians were forced to live on reservations or move to Canada.

For the next 150 years, the United States Government treated all Indians with dishonor and dishonesty. It was not until 1924 that Indians were recognized as citizens of the United States. Since then, Native Americans have gradually gained the respect and rights to which they are entitled.

Despite years of hardship and mistreatment, the Iroquois Nation has not vanished. Today there are more than 50,000 Iroquois, living mostly in northern New York State and southern Canada.

Before the White Men

THE STORY of the Iroquois Indians begins long before the white explorers, traders, and settlers reached the shores of the New World. The Iroquois originally lived in some unknown part of North America. According to legend, these Indians were instructed by the Great Spirit to move into the Northeast. There they carved a territory for themselves in the middle of a rival group of Indians, the Algonquins.

The Iroquois settled in the beautiful and rich lands of northern New York State. We know this territory today as the area surrounding Lake Ontario, the five Finger Lakes, and the Saint Lawrence River. The lakes and rivers provided abundant fish. Thick woods offered game of many kinds. It was an ideal location. But the Iroquois had to fight their neighbors to maintain this new homeland.

Fighting became a way of life for the Iroquois in those centuries before the arrival of the white men. In fact, the word "Iroquois" is the Algonquin word meaning "rattlesnake." That name tells us how the enemy viewed the Iroquois. The first white men learned of the Iroquois from rival Indians who lived along the Atlantic coast. The Iroquois called themselves "Hodenosaunee" (Hō-dē-nō-saw-ne), meaning "the people of the longhouse."

The Iroquois Indians are not one tribe but several. The group includes the Mohawk, the Seneca, the Onondaga, the Oneida, and the Cayuga tribes. Today these names mark well-known areas of New York and the Northeast. The Iroquois became a Nation of six tribes after 1715 when the Tuscarora Indians relocated from the south to join them.

The Iroquois were constantly fighting. They fought to defend themselves from their enemies. They fought to gain more land or more power. But they also fought to avenge themselves in intertribal feuds. The Iroquois fought as often with each other as they did with unrelated tribes.

The young Indian male was trained for fighting from boyhood. In winter, he lived alone in the woods with only a bow, arrow, hatchet, and knife to defend himself against wolves and wildcats. The young man also consumed drinks made from deadly herbs to prove his strength to fight off evil. He became a "brave" after he passed all the tests. Then he was allowed to join the warriors of his tribe.

The Seneca and the Mohawk tribes were the most fierce among the Iroquois Nation. Their warriors conducted many raids upon other Iroquois tribes as well as upon the rival Algonquin and Huron. As raiders, they could approach like foxes, fight like lions, and disappear like birds. They were masters of the silent ambush in the woods.

In a Seneca village, the formation of a war party was announced when a brave would fling a hatchet into the war post in the center of the village. This was a sign for the other men to get ready for battle. It was also a sign for the women, who would prepare rations of dried corn and maple sugar for the men to take on the raid.

On the night before a raid, the war chief of a village summoned the warriors to an assembly called a powwow. There they danced and prayed in preparation for their battle. Before dawn, they silently crept through the woods to the place of attack. Sometimes they traveled for days to reach their destination. The warriors let out horrible shrieks to announce the opening moment of the raid.

The raiders used burning arrows to set the village on fire. Often the raiders took scalps of other Indians. Sometimes it was done to prove their success. Other times, they took scalps to show revenge for some terrible offense that caused a long-lasting feud. Frequently, the raiders took other Indians as captives. Women and children prisoners were adopted into a tribe. Often male prisoners became replacements for husbands who had been killed in other battles. Some male captives were tortured and killed.

The conquering Mohawk and Seneca Indians tortured a captive by tying him to a pole in the center of the village. Then a fire was lighted at the base of the pole, and the captive slowly roasted to death. A truly courageous Indian never showed his pain or fear.

The Iroquois developed a powerful war club for close combat. It was usually carved from a single piece of hard wood. It had a rounded head and a long curved handle. The tip of the handle was sometimes shaped like the face of an animal. A warrior using this club could split a skull with a single blow.

Their skills as warriors would make the Iroquois the dominant force in the Northeast after the 1570s. But before that time, they nearly destroyed themselves by the constant warfare among the five tribes that then comprised the Iroquois Nation.

The League of the Iroquois Nation

After centuries of continuous family warfare, the Iroquois were finally united in a "great peace." According to legend, a holy man by the name of Deganawidah conceived the idea of a union of the five Iroquois tribes. He had a vision of the tribes united under the sheltering branches of a great tree. At the top of the tree rested a gigantic eagle that would warn the Iroquois of approaching enemies.

A Mohawk Indian by the name of Hiawatha heard of Deganawidah's vision and strongly believed that peace could happen. Hiawatha traveled from village to village, from tribe to tribe, spreading the message of peace. This took several years, but Hiawatha was finally successful in his mission. Do not confuse this man named Hiawatha, sometimes spelled Hayontawatha, with the Indian in Longfellow's poem of the same name. That Hiawatha was a fictional character.

In 1570, the Mohawk, Seneca, Onondaga, Oneida, and Cayuga tribes formed a confederacy called the League of the Iroquois, or the League of the Five Nations. It was the first form of democracy in the New World. This happened fifty years before the Pilgrims landed in Plymouth Colony in Massachusetts.

Under the rules of the League, each of the five tribes continued to govern itself. It was the task of the Great Council of the League to confer about problems with outside tribes. This governing body was made up of 50 members. Each tribe of the Iroquois Nation had a certain number of Council members. That number has remained the same to this

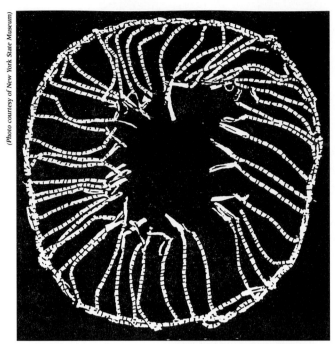

The string record
of the Iroquois League.

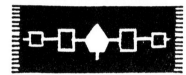

Hayontawatha Belt—a peace
sign between the five nations.

day. After the death of Hiawatha, his seat on the Council was never filled by another Mohawk. None felt worthy enough to take Hiawatha's place.

The founding of the League was recorded for posterity by a special circle of wampum strings, made with 1,800 beads. Wampum was the name for Indian beads which were originally made from sea shells. The Iroquois and other Eastern Indians used wampum for official events. (See the chapter on Wampum for more about this topic.)

The circle of wampum strings looks like a sun with 50 rays turned inward. It is a symbol of the equality of the members of the League. The outer rim of the circle was made by twisting two strings together. One string stands for the

League's Great Peace; the other string stands for its Great Law.

The 50 rays of the circle represent the members of the Council. One ray is longer than the rest. That signifies the Onondaga "Keeper of the Wampum" who was entrusted with the safety and heritage of all League wampum. After the American Revolution, this piece of history was moved to Canada. It is now displayed in the National Museum of Canada.

The Great Council met each year in Onondaga territory (near what is now Syracuse, New York) on a high hill where the Tree of Great Peace stood. A fire burned at the site throughout the meeting. In the 1600s a wampum belt was made to commemorate the founding of

The old Council House, Portage, N.Y.

*Thayendanegea, captain
of the six nations.*

the League. The belt shows four squares and a pine tree connected to one another. The tree represents the Onondaga land where the Council met. The squares represent the four other tribes of the Iroquois Nation. This belt is now displayed in the New York State Museum at Albany.

The members of the Great Council were males, but they were selected by the female who headed each *clan* or family. The Iroquois, like many other Indian groups, gave great power to women. The Iroquois women made the decisions about important matters. They briefed the Council members before each session, checked their work in the Council, and, when necessary, removed a member from office.

Each member of the Great Council was

called a *sachem*. A sachem needed great skills of communication and persuasion, much like the members of the United States Congress. Each sachem had the opportunity to stand before the Council and express his concern about a problem, usually a problem with an Algonquin enemy. When a decision had to be made on an issue, all members had to agree before action was taken.

The five tribes belonging to the League lived in peace with one another for many years. They hoped their league would be the beginning of a confederacy that would one day include all the Indian tribes around them. But that never happened. One tribe, the Tuscarora, did join the League in 1715. The confederacy was then known as the League of Six Nations.

People of the Longhouse

The Iroquois Indians are famous for the style of house they developed. Called the *longhouse,* it was a long and narrow building that could be from 50 to 150 feet long and from 18 to 25 feet wide. The roof was arched. The walls, formed by curved poles, were covered with sheets of bark. The longhouse had no windows.

Many families of one clan lived in one longhouse. Each family had only a small space, probably not much more than that of a large bunk bed of today. The family "bunk" was part of two continuous platforms, one above the other, built along each wall. On the lower platform, the whole family slept together under a blanket of bearskin. On the upper level, the family stored its possessions: pots, cradleboards, and weapons.

A central hallway ran the length of the longhouse. Small fires burned at many sites along this open space. Two families shared each fire for cooking, as well as

warmth and light. Smoke from these fires curled upward and out of the building through smoke holes in the roof. When it rained or snowed, these holes were closed.

Each longhouse was governed by a woman. When an Iroquois couple married, they went to live in the longhouse of the wife's family. All property belonged to the Iroquois woman, and all power came from her.

Each Iroquois village had many longhouses, depending on the number of people living in the village. A village, usually located high on a river bank, was surrounded with a *palisade* — a high fence made of pointed, slender tree trunks. A warrior would stand guard on the palisade day and night.

As a village was being built, the land between the palisade and the river was cleared of all low growing bushes and trees. This gave the Indians protection because they could easily spot any approaching raiders.

A village had a life of about 10 years. After that the farm lands around the village were no longer fertile. The people of

the village would then move on to a new location.

On the cleared land, the Indian women planted crops of corn, squash, beans, tobacco, and sunflowers. Like other woodland Indians, the Iroquois women also collected wild nuts, fruits, and berries. They made teas from herbs, plants, and some trees. One favorite tea was made from the sap of the maple tree. Sometimes the tea was seasoned with sassafras root.

Because the Iroquois lived in areas that had long and harsh winters, the women had to store food to last through the cold times. Dried corn and other vegetables were placed in a deep pit that was lined and covered with bark. A final cover of earth secured the stored vegetables. Meat was stored in a similar way, except deer skins were used to line and cover the pits.

In the late fall and early winter, the Iroquois men spent many weeks hunting for game to supply the village with meat for the year ahead. The forests were abundant with deer, bear, wild fowl, and other small animals. The men used blow guns with small spears when hunting squirrels and birds. But for large game, the Indians used the bow and arrow. Frequently, the Indians trapped a large number of deer before killing them.

Deer hunting was an important task for all Eastern Indians. Iroquois villages were often abandoned for several months while all the families went with the men to the hunting grounds. The deer provided the members of a village with both food and skins. Many items of Iroquois clothing were made from this animal.

In cold weather, the men wore a tunic-like shirt with fringed edges. In both cold and warm weather, they wore leggings, seamed up the front, without fringe. The seams of the leggings were covered with fancy stitches, like embroidery. The leggings reached down to the top of the moccasins and often dragged on the ground. For special occasions, the men wore a short kilt over the leggings.

In warm weather, men usually wore just leggings and a *breechclout*. A breechclout was a piece of fabric about 18 inches wide that passed between the legs. It was held at the waist by a belt and hung down to the knees in front and back. After the arrival of the white man, the Iroquois male began to carry a tobacco pouch. It hung at his waist and was attached to a shoulder strap that crossed his chest.

The Iroquois man sometimes wore an unusual feather-covered cap. It fit closely to the shape of his head, much like a knit cap of today. And in the center of the hat, one or two feathers stood straight up.

Many men, especially the warriors, cut off most of their hair. They left a lock or tuft that stood up in the center and back

of the head. This was called a "roach." One or two feathers were added for decoration. This Iroquois style has been adapted in a haircut style, called "the Mohawk," worn by teenage boys in recent times.

Iroquois women wore their hair long and braided. Their clothing was simple — deerskin skirts that fell below the knees, and leggings like the men's. In cold weather they added a loose cape-like blouse with deep fringes along the edges.

Corn—The Staple of Life

Like most Indians of the East, the Iroquois depended upon corn as their main source of food. They ate corn in soups, in breads, and in puddings. Corn and beans made succotash, a favorite food. Corn was served with greens and nuts. It was flavored with berries or maple sugar.

The Indians of the longhouse usually ate one meal a day, about mid-morning. But a pot of food was always on the fire, and people ate when they got hungry.

The corn plant provided more than food. The Indians used the whole plant for various things. The husks were perfect for making dolls for the children. The doll's head was always faceless because the Iroquois believed if a doll had a face, it might turn into a real person.

Corn husks were also woven into many kinds of mats. Husks were even braided to make a hammock for a baby's bed that hung inside the family bunk in the longhouse. During the daytime, a baby was strapped in a cradleboard that the mother carried on her back or hung from a low branch of a tree.

The Indians even found a use for the corn cob. It was made into a pipe, a back scratcher, a scrubber, and many more things. Dried cobs were burned to smoke fish and meat.

13

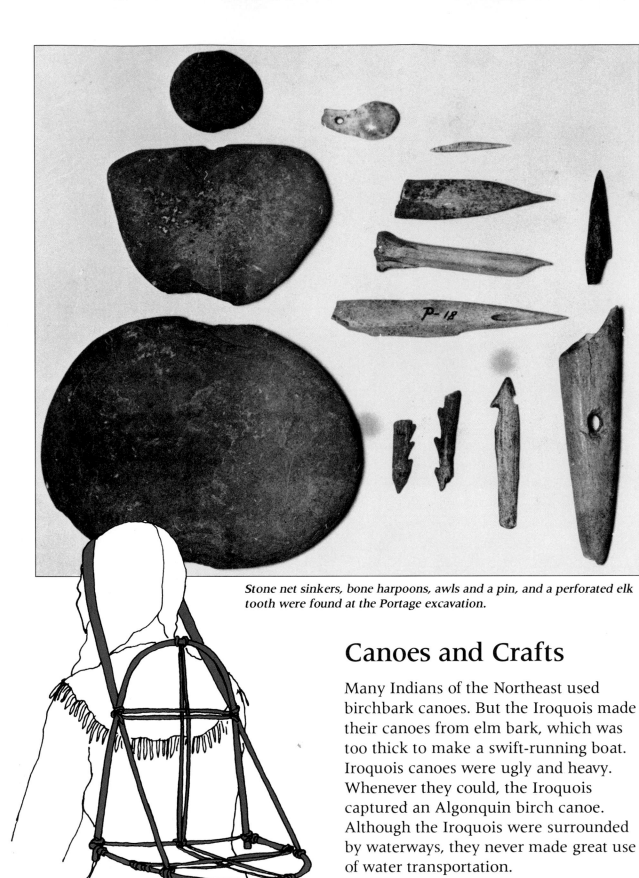

Stone net sinkers, bone harpoons, awls and a pin, and a perforated elk tooth were found at the Portage excavation.

Burden carrier.

Canoes and Crafts

Many Indians of the Northeast used birchbark canoes. But the Iroquois made their canoes from elm bark, which was too thick to make a swift-running boat. Iroquois canoes were ugly and heavy. Whenever they could, the Iroquois captured an Algonquin birch canoe. Although the Iroquois were surrounded by waterways, they never made great use of water transportation.

One craft that seems unique to the Iroquois is a "burden carrier." It was a

Cayuga tomahawk pipe.
(Photo courtesy of Buffalo and Erie County Historical Society)

(Photo courtesy of Buffalo and Erie County Historical Society)

Kienka brass kettle.

Metal bracelet.
(Photo courtesy of Buffalo and Erie County Historical Society)

Pottery pipe.

Photo courtesy of Buffalo and Erie County Historical Society

frame made of hickory and basswood fibers. The woman usually carried it on her back and secured it by long straps around her head or shoulders. A variation of this carrier was used by mothers to carry a baby. Then the carrier was called a *cradleboard.*

Iroquois women made clay pots for cooking and storage. The clay pots had round bodies and raised, square collars or rims. Geometric line patterns were often etched on the collars. After the arrival of the white men, the women bartered for the sturdy brass kettles to replace the clay pots.

The pottery pipe is another craft that was unique to the Iroquois before the white men. The pipes were smaller than most Indian pipes and were not used as ceremonial pipes. They were just for enjoying a smoke. The bowl and stem of the pipe were made in one piece. An animal's face or some design often decorated the pipe.

Wampum—Beads That Talked

When the word wampum is mentioned, people often think of Indian money. It is true that wampum was used like money to barter for goods. But that happened in the 1600s after the Dutch set up trading posts along the Hudson River. Originally, Indians of the Atlantic coast developed wampum and used it for historical and religious purposes.

Wampum was the name for the tube-like beads Indians made from sea shells. White wampum beads were made from the inside of a conch or whelk — a large saltwater univalve. Purple wampum came from the quahog — a saltwater clam. Purple wampum was the most valuable because it was harder to find the shell from which it was made.

In the Iroquois Nation, certain Indians were the official wampum makers. Making wampum was a special skill. First the unwanted parts of a shell had to be trimmed away with a stone tool. Next, a small hole was drilled into a rounded piece of shell. This required the efforts of two people: one to hold the shell and one to drill the hole. A sharp, slender piece of bone was probably used as the drill. While one person held the shell, the other person rotated the drill back and forth between his open-palmed hands. Once the hole was made, the bead was polished with rough sand.

Wampum eventually came in many colors. But it was not Indian-made wampum. It was wampum manufactured by the Dutch and other European traders and settlers.

The Iroquois, like other Indians, had no written language in the time before the white men. But they were still able

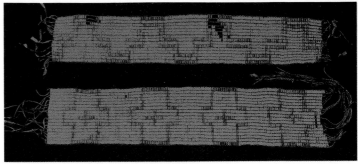

(Photo courtesy of Buffalo and Erie County Historical Society)

Wampum belts were used as money.

to send important messages and record important events for their descendants. Wampum was their form of paper and books. They shaped wampum strings and formed designs on wampum belts that told a story. Of course, not everyone could understand the words and ideas sealed in the wampum shapes.

Each tribe had an official Keeper of the Wampum. It was his sacred job to memorize the message of each wampum belt or string. The Keeper first learned the story in the wampum from the chief or sachem who ordered the making of the wampum. Each time the story was told, the Keeper listened carefully so he could repeat each word exactly as it was first spoken.

To preserve the history of the wampum, each Keeper trained an apprentice who would one day become the next Keeper of the Wampum. The Keeper was the link between the past and the future. His was a very important and honored position. In times of danger, the wampum was buried. When the danger passed, the Keeper unearthed the valuable beads.

Wampum told the story of not only a tribe's history, but also its customs and laws. The founding of the League of the Iroquois was carefully documented in wampum. That is explained in the chapter on the League.

Masks from the False Face Society.

(Photo by courtesy of Buffalo and Erie County Historical Society)

The False Face Society

Ceremonies and festivals were important in the lives of the Iroquois. Most of these events were held to honor the Great Spirit who provided good crops and plenty of game. Some ceremonies were held to scare off the Evil Spirit. Members of the False Face Society did yearly combat with the spirit who made people ill.

A sick person often had a dream in which someone wearing a grotesque mask appeared. When this happened, the family of the sick person called upon the False Face Society for help to perform healing ceremonies.

Members of the society wore large, ugly, carved masks when they came to the longhouse of the sick person. They also carried noisemakers made of turtle shells filled with pebbles. They danced around the sick person, chanted, rattled the noisemakers, and sprinkled tobacco ashes over the ailing one.

Once the sick person was cured, he became a member of the False Face Society. His first task was to carve his own mask. According to legend, the design of the mask had to be the same as the face he saw in his dream. Sup-

posedly, each mask had different features. The mouth, for example, might be crooked or straight-lipped, or it might be open with the tongue sticking out.

The mask was carved upon a living basswood tree. While the carver worked on the face, a priest of the Society chanted in front of the tree. He was calling the spirit of the "flying head" to enter the face in the tree. When the carver was finished, the tree was cut down. The carver took the face home and continued to shape the face so it could be worn as a mask. He added hair and painted the face black or red.

The Indians believed the mask was a living thing that had to be respected and protected. Each mask was a commemoration of the original False Face — a mythical creature who had been punished by the Great Spirit for being too boastful and proud. His punishment was to spend eternity healing the sick.

Members of the False Face Society performed another task. In spring and fall they entered each longhouse where they conducted a ceremony to scare away the spirits of illness.

19

Fur Trade with the White Men

When the Dutch, French, and English discovered the great variety and quantity of fur-bearing animals in the New World, they were eager to trade with the Indians for fur. And the Indians were eager to obtain the wonderful possessions of the white men: metal pots and kettles, steel needles, jewels, woven cloth and blankets. And guns!

The Europeans wanted all the fur the Indians could bring them. Before the arrival of the white men, Indians killed animals only to provide food and clothing for their families. They were careful to leave enough of each kind of animal to breed more for another year. But that care ended as they became more greedy for the European goods of the strangers who were invading Indians lands.

In the early 1600s the Europeans traded for fur with the coastal Indian tribes, but after a few years those Indians had exhausted their source of fur. Then the white men moved inland and encountered the Iroquois.

Like other tribes before them, the Iroquois also became greedy and killed off

too many animals. But the Iroquois had an easy solution to their dilemma. They invaded the territory of their rivals who lived further west and north. They went on the warpath.

Because the five tribes of the Iroquois Nation were good warriors and well organized, they easily conquered their neighbors — the Huron and Algonquin. By 1644 the Iroquois League controlled the territory from the St. Lawrence River to Tennessee and from New England to Michigan.

They controlled travel on the rivers and the Great Lakes. Often they seized boatloads of fur from other Indians. the Iroquois eventually collected *tribute* — gifts and payments for protection — from the tribes within their new territory. No conquered tribe made any agreements with the white men without the approval of the Iroquois.

Between 1650 and 1685, the Iroquois League maintained a general peace throughout their territory. By the 1700s the Iroquois were drawn more and more into the rivalry between the French and British. That rivalry eventually split the League and destroyed the power of the Iroquois.

"Braddock's Defeat," a painting by Elwin Willard Deming, depicts a scene from a battle during the French and Indian Wars.

(Photo courtesy of Buffalo and Erie County Historical Society)

The French and British Rivalry

The Iroquois played a major role in helping the British defeat the French in North America. If the French had not made early enemies of the Iroquois, the history of the United States might have a heavy French influence rather than English.

In 1615, the soldiers of the French explorer, Samuel de Champlain, attacked an Onondaga village and killed many Indians. This was the beginning of the Iroquois hatred for the French.

In 1644, the Iroquois extended their control to the area that is now Montreal, Canada. After that both the French and British carefully courted the Iroquois for future support. But the Iroquois League wisely resisted supporting either group.

However, that attitude changed over the next one hundred years. The Iroquois drifted gradually to the support of the British king and his colonists who were frequently at war with the French.

During the French and Indian War (1755-1763), many Indian tribes in the East sided with the French. That's how the war got its name; it was a war of the French and Indians against the British. But a few tribes supported the British.

Some of the tribes of the Iroquois Nation unofficially became allies of the British.

It was because of an Irish man named William Johnson that the Iroquois supported the British forces. Johnson was a fur trader who settled in the Mohawk territory and became very friendly with

22

the Iroquois. In fact, he twice married Mohawk women. His second wife was Molly Brant.

Johnson was placed in charge of Indian Affairs by the British king and soon became one of the largest landowners in colonial America. In 1755 when war started, Johnson appeared at a Great Council meeting of the League and asked for volunteer fighters. Many Mohawk volunteered, and many were killed in battle. That was a serious event for the Iroquois. In the future, they would always favor the British over the French.

The Albany Congress of 1754

In 1754, the British realized the French and Indian War was inevitable. They called a meeting of the important colonial leaders at Albany, New York. The most famous colonial leader who attended was Benjamin Franklin. The British also invited 150 Iroquois chiefs in hopes that they would sign an agreement to support the British when war broke out.

But the Iroquois made no agreement. Moreover, they scolded the British for letting the French get such a strong hold West of the Hudson River. The Indians feared for their own well being in the presence of so many French.

Chief Hendrick of the Mohawks angrily stated: "The French are men. They fortify everywhere. But you are like women . . . you have thrown us behind your back and disregarded us." To pacify the Indians, the British gave them 30 wagonloads of presents, including guns.

At this meeting, Benjamin Franklin tried to organize the British colonists and the king into a confederacy that would give them strength, like the League gave strength and unity to the Iroquois. Franklin failed, but he would raise his plan again, after the Revolutionary War had separated King George III from North America.

Joseph Brant, Mohawk Sachem

One Indian had a large part in bringing the Iroquois into the American Revolution. His name was Joseph Brant.

Thayandaneca was his Indian name. He was the younger brother of Molly Brant who had married William Johnson, the British Superintendent of Indian Affairs. Joseph was raised partly with the whites. He attended a colonial school in Lebanon, Connecticut, where he learned to speak, read, and write English.

After the colonists declared their independence from England in 1776, the Great Council of the Iroquois League met to make an important decision. Should they take sides in the coming war, or should they remain neutral? It was Joseph Brant who stood firmly on the side of the British King.

After long days of debate, the Mohawk, Seneca, Cayuga, and Onondaga tribes sided with Brant in his support of the British. The Oneida and the Tuscarora wanted to support the colonists.

The members of the Great Council could not agree on one course of action. It meant that the League would take no offical part in the Revolutionary War. But the four tribes who favored support for the King took up arms and fought with the British soldiers.

Brant was made a colonel in the British Army and commanded the forces of the Iroquois. They fought along side the soldiers of General Burgoyne. Even with the help of the Iroquois, Burgoyne's men were defeated at Saratoga, New York, in 1777. It was the turning point in the war. After that, the forces of General George Washington gained more and more victories.

Joseph Brant.

The final defeat of the British was also a final defeat for the Iroquois Nation. They paid a high price for supporting the losing side in the war. The Iroquois were forced to surrender control of their lands to the new government of the United States.

In 1784, the Iroquois signed the Treaty of Fort Stanwix (near the present site of Rome, New York). They gave up several million acres of land in return for approximately 100,000 acres of reservation lands in New York.

Before the Revolutionary War ended, Brant fled to Canada. From there he sailed to England to plead for help for his people. Brant knew the Indians would have to sacrifice their valuable lands in New York. But he persuaded the King to give to the Iroquois lands in Canada as valuable as those they would lose in the United States.

The King granted to Brant a large tract of land in Ontario, Canada. Today it is called Brant County; it is still home to many Mohawk Indians and other descendants of the Iroquois Nation.

Flintstone tools.

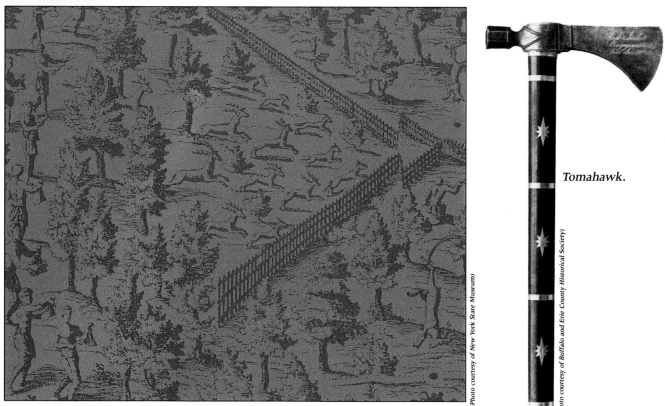

The Iroquois hunted by driving game into a trap.

Tomahawk.

The Legacy of the Iroquois League

The League of the Iroquois Nation is often referred to as The Confederacy. That is the title Benjamin Franklin used for the remarkable political organization formed by the Indians.

From 1736 to 1762, Franklin published information for the colonists about the Native Americans. He wrote frequently about the Iroquois Nation. Franklin greatly admired the unity and structure of their Confederacy.

What was known at that time about the laws of the Iroquois Nation was due to the work of a friend of Franklin, Cadwallader Colden, who wrote *The History of the Five Nations* in 1727. Colden had attended many meetings with the Iroquois and recorded their quotes about their Great Law, which was the foundation of their Confederacy.

Benjamin Franklin made proposals for the structure of the union of the Colonies, and later, of the United States. He adapted many of those ideas from the Great Law of the Iroquois. There are several parallels between the two nations. The most significant is that both have three interconnected branches of government. In the U.S. Constitution, we call those branches the Judicial, the Executive, and the Legislative.

The Iroquois have been called the Romans of North America. That title compares them to the ancient Romans who knew the importance of a strong political structure built upon a foundation of laws.

The Iroquois Today

The Iroquois have not vanished. Today there are more than 28,000 living in New York State — on or off reservations. And in Canada there are another 30,000 or more, mostly Mohawk descendants. A few thousand are scattered across the United States.

As far back as the 1600s, the Indians began to marry European traders and settlers. Gradually the Indians adopted many of the ways of the white men, especially their style of dress and housing. By the time the Treaty of Fort Stanwix was signed in 1784, the Iroquois were living in individual log houses instead of longhouses. Women wore calico dresses, and men wore trousers. The old Indian ways were almost gone.

Life on reservations during the 1800s and into the 1900s was often very difficult. The Indians survived by raising their own food and providing for all their needs. Some small amounts of money and other provisions were contributed by the U.S. Government and the State of New York.

The Iroquois survived better than Indians on western reservations. They maintained their Great Council which continued to meet, according to tradition, in Onondaga territory. And the Mohawk men developed a new job skill.

In 1886, the Mohawk men of the Iroquois Nation became the first Indian steelworkers. They were hired to work on the construction of a bridge over the St. Lawrence River connecting Canada and the United States. Although they were hired to work on the ground, they soon began to work on the highest and most dangerous beams.

The white steelworkers discovered that the Mohawks had no fear of being perched high up in the windy sky over a roaring river far below. They would run up, down, over, and across high beams as if they were running on the ground.

There are probably two reasons why these Indians adapted so easily to working on high steel bridge girders. Young boys of all Iroquois tribes were encouraged to climb the tallest pine tree around and stay there as long as possible. It was a test of bravery.

The second reason has to do with the way an Iroquois walks. It is said that an Iroquois walks with one foot directly in front of the other, in a straight line. His footprints in the snow would look like only one foot. The white man's path would show two prints.

The Mohawk men also proved to be quite skilled at handling the heavy and noisy riveting gun that bridgemen must use to bolt the girders together. This job skill was then, and now, a highly paid career field. The first Mohawk bridgemen taught other Iroquois the new skill. And they in turn taught still more. The men of the Iroquois Nation have worked on most of the famous bridges built since 1886.

They have worked not only in the United States and Canada, but in many parts of the world. As bridgemen, the Iroquois men continue to display their Indian courage as warriors of the steel girders.

In the past 40 years, Iroquois descendants work everywhere. They may be in offices or factories, in schools or hospitals, in laboratories or farm fields. These Native Americans and Canadians have a proud past and a strong future.

Important Dates in Iroquois History

1570	The Mohawk, Seneca, Onondaga, Oneida, and Cayuga tribes unite to form the League of the Iroquois Nation.
1600s	Iroquois begin trading furs with the Dutch, French and British.
1615	Soldiers of Samuel de Champlain attack Onondaga Village.
1644	Iroquois extend their control throughout most of Northeast.
1650-1685	Iroquois maintain peace with neighboring tribes.
1715	Tuscarora tribe joins League of the Iroquois Nation.
1754	Great Albany Congress — British fail to gain official support from the Iroquois against the French.
1755-1763	William Johnson persuades the Mohawks to unofficially fight for the British in the French and Indian War.
1776	Great Council of the League votes to remain neutral in the American Revolutionary War.
1776	Joseph Brant, Mohawk Chief, persuades Iroquois to unofficially fight with the British in the Revolutionary War.
1777	Defeat of the British and Iroquois at Saratoga, New York.
1784	Treaty of Fort Stanwix — Iroquois surrender their lands in the Northeast for reservations in New York; many Indians move to Canada.
1886	Mohawk Indians begin long heritage as bridge builders.

INDEX

KEY WEST

BY GERALD SPRAYREGEN

DEDICATION TO:

Frances (Gordon) Sprayregen   1907–1996
Herman Sprayregen   1898–1980

Parents of: Carol, Gerald, and Seymour   Grandparents of: David, Nicholas, Lisa, Pamela, and Sharon

Great Grandparents of: Nicole, Matthew, Melanie, Emily, Jesse, Jonathan, Benjamin, Nicole, and Alexa

1934

*A day never passes when I do not reflect on my mother's smile, beauty, sense of humor and gentleness,
my father's wisdom and strength, and the love I received from both of them. GS*

ACKNOWLEDGMENT

My sincere thanks to the following individuals and organizations for their help, advice and suggestions in helping me create *Key West*: Bob Cardenas, Tom McCarrain, Sam Trophia, Mark Prokopeak, Kelly Tavares, Buck Banks, Norman Aberele, Norman Woods, Sr., Betty Sammis, Nancy Forester, Joe Allen, Paul Collins, Jacque Sands, Dan Burley, Peter Green, Donna Edward, Carol Wrightman, Gharavi Mohammad, Sharon Wells, Winifred Shine Fryzel, Renee Onorato, John Brancati, John Miller, Paul Hause, Gerard Nudo, and R.R. Donnelley.

My grateful appreciation and special thanks to the following for their suggestions and information, which have all been incorporated into *Key West*: Mel Cowher, Tom Tong, Wendy Xu, Heather Peres, and Dr. Seymour Sprayregen.

I am forever indebted to Gloria Sophia who spent many months working on this project with me while simultaneously devoting hundreds of hours to typing the various drafts of the manuscript for Key West.

BIBLIOGRAPHY

Papa – Hemingway in Key West
– James McLendon
Langley Press, Inc.- 1972 revised -1990

Key West Houses – Leslie Linsley
Rizzoli N.Y. - 1992

Key West – History of an Island of Dreams
– Maureen Ogle
University Press of Florida - 2003

The Houses of Key West – Alex Caemmerer
Pineapple Press, Sarasota, Fl. - 1992

Walking and Biking Guide
 – to Historic Key West – Sharon Wells,
Sharon Wells Company, Key West, Fl.- 2003

Key West Gardens and Their Stories
 – Janis Frawley-Holler,
Pineapple Press, Sarasota, Fl. – 2000

Shell's Key West Classics and Challenge –
2003

Key Wester – Katharine Roach
Gorden B. Brown, Jr. – April 2003

First printing - December 2003
Second printing - May 2004
Published by
Gerald Sprayregen Productions
10 Southeastern Farms Road
Pound Ridge, New York 10576
914-234-2618

Printed and bound by R.R. Donnelley – China
ISBN: 0-9746299-0-1
Library of Congress Catalog
Card Number: 2003097592

TABLE OF CONTENTS

THE GRAND DAMES OF KEY WEST

GARDENS OF KEY WEST

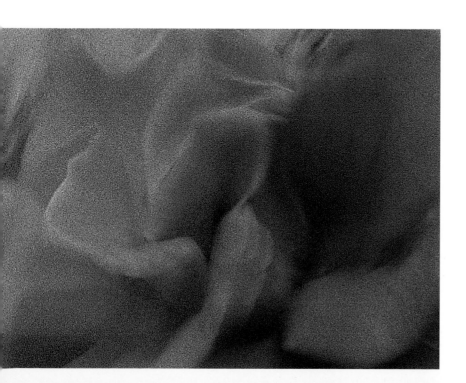

Key West, with its fascinating 28,000 citizens, is a tropical paradise, squeezed between the Gulf of Mexico and the Atlantic Ocean, at the southernmost tip of the United States. Key West is only 90 miles from Cuba and 150 miles from Miami. The island itself, roughly two by four miles, is partially surrounded by live coral reefs, which are so unique they attract people from all over the world.

Key West has a intriguing history, because of its inhabitants, its climate, and its hype. It keeps reinventing itself, much to the displeasure of the conchs, a nickname given to anything original to Key West.

Key West has a long and colorful past, beginning with its European discovery in 1815 by Ponce de Leon. The island was originally known as Cayo Hueso (Isle of Bones) because it was littered with remains from an Indian battlefield. Unfortunately, the majority of archeological artifacts have been lost or destroyed by time. The name Key West is the English translation of the Spanish name.

In 1821, John Simonton purchased Key West for $2,000 from Jean Pablo Solas. Solas had received the property in 1815 from the Spanish Government for favors he had performed years earlier.

In 1821, Andrew Jackson led a group of Americans to Pensacola, Florida to witness the transfer of Florida from the Spanish government to the United States. A short time later, a naval base was established there, to try to stop pirates. Since 1821, the presence of the US Navy has been a major factor in the growth and development of Key West, which was incorporated in 1828.

In the 1800s, pirates ruled the seas around Florida, stopping any ships they could find, taking their valuable cargo, and often killing all passengers and crewmembers. Because of this, the owners of merchant vessels demanded action. Congress responded in 1822 by ordering that all pirates be eradicated in the Florida area. Commander David Porter was put in charge of a squad of ships and 1,100 men. Porter turned the tables on the pirates, burning their ships and killing the pirates who did not flee the area. In less than two years, all pirates were eliminated. It is estimated that there were 100 people in Key West in 1823, and by 1830 this increased to over 500, brave, hearty souls. During these early years, Key West was branded as a place for drinkers, killers, and in general, an unsavory place. This reputation only seemed to increase the interest of many Americans, who are basically imbued with a pioneering spirit.

During the early 19th century, all ships carrying cargo between Cuba and the United States had to attempt to outmaneuver the dangerous reef-filled waters, which held Key West captive. This particular set of circumstances created a utopia for the New England seamen, who along with the Bahamians, created Key West's first major industry, that of salvaging cargo from the treacherous coral reefs. Many of the early homes of Key West were built and furnished utilizing the spoils of these shipwrecks. For approximately 25 years the salvage industry flourished, but as lighthouses became more common, the salvage business lost its profitability.

The sponge industry began in the 1840s, and is the only major industry started in the 19th century in Key West which has continued to survive and prosper. Fortunately for the Key West sponge industry, there are a number of fields such as the medical field, which need fibers of natural sponges.

Sunset Key

In the late 1800s, many Cubans were leaving Cuba because of the Spanish-Cuban territorial wars. Since Key West was only 90 miles away, it attracted the Cubans, who arrived with their cigar-making experience. The first cigar factory was opened in 1831, and by 1890 there were over 150 separate cigar factories in Key West. The cigar industry created thousands of jobs for the 17,000 residents of Key West. In the early 1900s, because of labor unrest, many cigar makers moved to Tampa, Florida. In 1880, Key West had the distinction of having more inhabitants than any other city in Florida, and was also the richest city per capita in the United States. In 1890, the population of Florida was 700,000 people.

In 1905, Henry Flagler, co-founder with John D. Rockefeller of Standard Oil, announced plans to build a railroad from Miami to Key West, which would link Key West to the rest of Florida. At that time, everyone and everything entering Key West came by ship because at that point there were neither roads nor rail into Key West. Flagler was the developer of Palm Beach, but this monumental undertaking was considered by many as Flagler's folly. There were over 40 bridges that had to be built, and one was seven miles long. The residents of Key West viewed these incredible plans with delight, and felt if that enormous undertaking were successful, it would make Key West more desirable than Miami or Palm Beach. The railroad from Miami to Key West was completed in seven years, covering over 140 miles of swampy wilderness and open seas, and cost over $125 million dollars. Over 200 men lost their lives during the construction of this monumental undertaking, due to hurricanes and other tragedies. Flagler died one year after its completion.

During the Great Depression in 1932, with the exception of "Papa" Hemmingway, and a few others, virtually every citizen in Key West was on relief. Key West was totally bankrupt and turned its charter back to the state and federal governments. President Roosevelt hired Julius Stone to save the city. Mr. Stone created a new tourist campaign which advertised Key West as "America's Bermuda." Millions of dollars were poured in by the Florida Emergency Relief Administration Fund. Attractions for Key West had to be built, and the first project was the first open-air aquarium in the country.

During the Second World War, Key West was the base of operations supporting naval destroyers and aircraft. In 1940, it became a training base. Shortly thereafter, President Harry S. Truman established his vacation home, "The Little White House" in Key West. Population more than doubled from 1940 to 1960, and tourism increased substantially. In 1960, there were approximately 50,000 people living in Key West, which included 20,000 military with their families and two to four thousand civilian employees. During the next 20 years the population decreased by 25%, due mainly to a cutback in naval personnel. Once again, the city re-emphasized tourism, as it did in the forties, and tourism became its major industry. During this time, Duval Street and Old Town were refurbished. Businesses were started and Key West, once again, became a popular place to visit. Many old homes were renovated, mostly by the gay population, and the value of property increased substantially. Today, Key West is an international destination, and home to more published authors per square mile than any other spot in America.

Atlantic Ocean

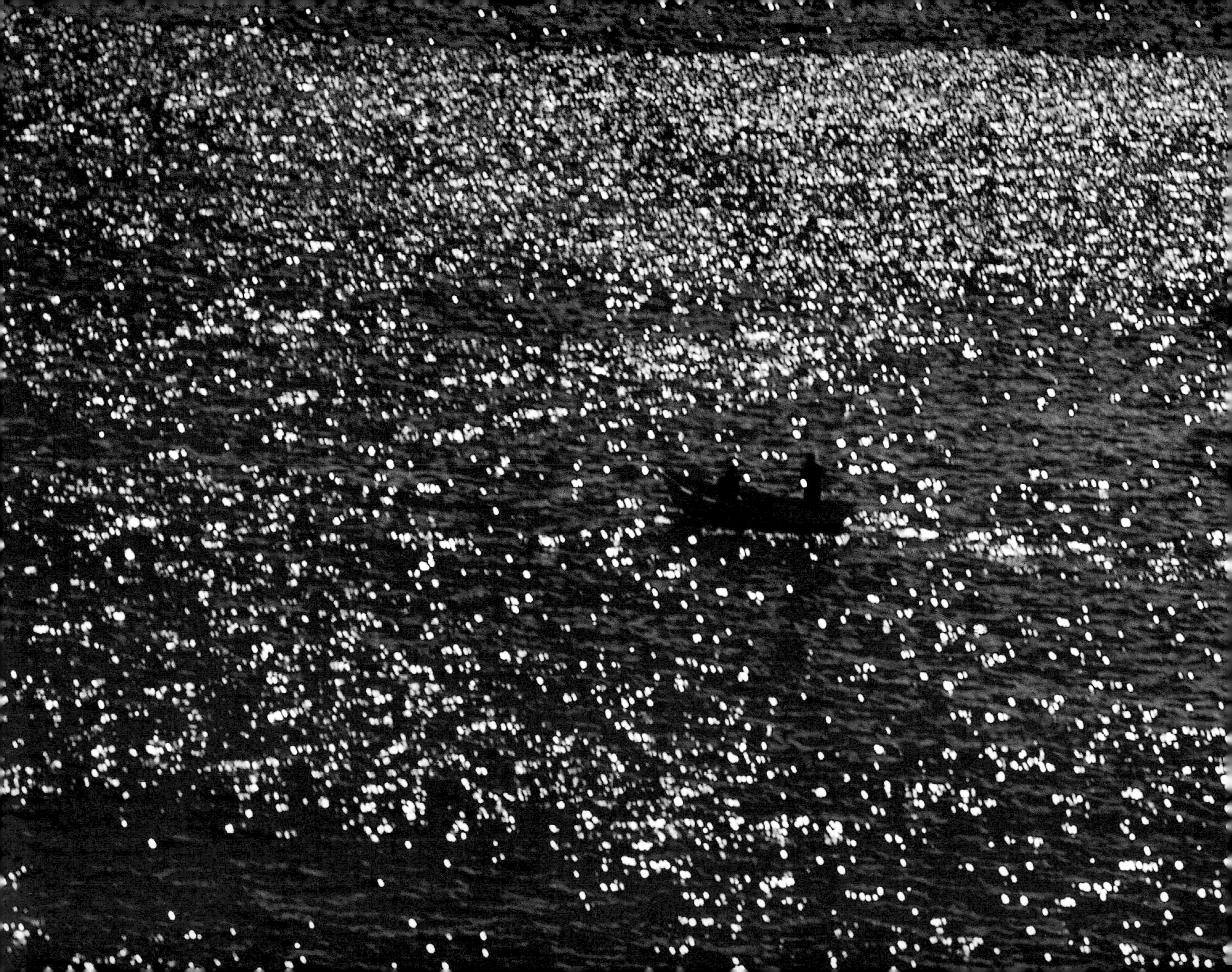

HOUSE BOATS
1801 North Roosevelt Boulevard

During the 1950s a number of houseboat owners sailed their vessels into Key West, found it to their liking, and tied up along South Roosevelt Boulevard at the Atlantic Ocean. Word spread, more houseboats arrived, and over the next number of years houseboats became a common sight on the Atlantic side of Key West. Since the houseboat owners were enjoying "squatters rights" (no rent), they decided to go one step further and plugged into the city's electrical system. Certainly from their point of view, free electricity was included in their squatters rights' package. The city of Key West felt a little differently, which is the cloth from which lawsuits are made. The city went to court to get rid of the squatters. The squatters liked "Paradise" and wanted to stay. The court battle went on for five decades. The squatters got older, some died and some new ones came, but the fight continued. Strangely enough, nature became the magistrate, and in 1998 hurricane George, while wreaking havoc on Key West, destroyed virtually all but a few of the houseboats. To add insult to injury for the poor squatters, the city finally got a court order forcing them to vacate. A few relocated to Garrison Bight, part of the city marina; some chose to seek their future elsewhere. Today there are approximately 88 "live-aboards" at Garrison Bight.

11

THE SHOT GUN HOUSE
411 Truman Avenue

During the late 19th Century "The Shot Gun House" became the prevailing home to be built in Key West. As cigar making rose to become the leading industry in Key West, it employed more than 5,000 individuals, which represented more than 16% of the population of the city. A need to build small inexpensive homes for the workers of the cigar factories arose. The Shot Gun House solved the problem perfectly. Originally conceived and built in West Africa, these homes were clustered together on a track of land and built quickly. These single-story, one-room wide buildings, were usually a set of three rooms, one behind the other, where, if a bullet were shot from the front doorway, it could pass through the house, out the back door, without touching a wall. There are numerous variations of this style, some quite sophisticated in design. These homes are constantly being restored and are quite desirable in Key West today.

E. H. GATO
JR. HOUSE
1327 Duval Street

This beautiful example of Victorian architecture (circa 1885), was built by Edward Hidalgo Gato for his son. The elder Gato left Cuba in the 1860s and became a legend in the Key West cigar industry.

Originally, this house was across the street facing South, but Mr. Gato was uncomfortable with the noonday heat on the porch, and so with the help of an army of mules, moved the house across the street. Interestingly enough, the street number 1327 never changed, and today it is the only odd-numbered house on that side of Duval Street. The house remained in the Gato family until the 1930s when it was sold. Today the E.H. Gato Jr. House is the southernmost guesthouse in the United States and is a very charming place to stay.

CATS

Make no mistake about it . . . Cats rule this Island! They go any place they want, sleep anywhere they find comfortable, gobble food indiscriminately off any table, and never, never get reprimanded. In the Hemingway Estate, there is a cat burial ground for approximately 60 cats, all previous inhabitants of 907 Whitehead Street. The cats were named after celebrities such as Spencer Tracy, Elizabeth Taylor and Shakespeare; currently the oldest living cat is Marilyn Monroe, age 19. Interestingly enough, at least half of the Hemingway cats are polydactyl (more than five toes).

Charlette is seated on this page and on the opposite page is Anna.

BICYCLES

The conch mode of transportation in Key West is the bicycle. No self-respecting resident would drive or walk to an island location if it could be reached by bicycle.

CARS

People who live in Key West year round are different. . . It is not 100% necessary to be a little eccentric, but if you are unconventional, odd, strange, bizarre, idiosyncratic, peculiar, whimsical, quirky, cranky, screwy, non-conformist, crackpot, oddball, weirdo, or a screwball, it would help.

19

KEY WEST SECESSION

If there is a single "high water mark" in the history of Key West, it is April 23, 1982. All Conchs point to that milestone day with pride because on that day Key West and the Florida Keys seceded from the U.S. and became the Conch Republic. A little history will explain this plan.

On April 18th, 1982, the U.S. Border Patrol set up a roadblock on U.S.I in Florida City to search all vehicles coming from Key West. This surprise barricade was set up on a Sunday afternoon as hundreds of visitors were leaving the Keys on the one and only road to Miami and the rest of the world. A 19 mile traffic jam developed, which prompted hundreds of calls to Key West Mayor Dennis Wardlow. Wardlow realized that if this roadblock continued, tourism would be incredibly diminished. The Border Patrol stated "We're checking on illegal aliens coming into the Keys," and later admitted, "drug interdiction" was the second motive. The Mayor and a group of delegates filed a federal injunction to force the Border Patrol to remove the roadblock. Unfortunately, the injunction was denied. On the way back from court in Miami, David Horan, the Key West attorney, while flying the delegates home to Key West, decided to aggressively buzz the roadblock and the Border Patrol. He was rewarded for his heroism by being named Secretary of the Conch Republic Air Force a few days later. On Friday, April 23rd, the day following the court's decision, the Conch Republic was born; its birthplace, Mallory Dock. Mayor Wardlow became Prime Minister, and ambassadors were appointed to Hawaii, Texas, and other important geographical locations.

Immediately, the new republic declared war on the United States, and its ships fired shots of conch fritters and old Cuban bread at navy personnel. Fortunately no one was injured, and within moments the new republic surrendered and requested millions of dollars in federal aid.

Thanks to the public relations work done by Stuart Newman, of Stuart Newman Associates, the entire episode received substantial media attention throughout the country. Each year the Key West declaration of independence is commemorated with a mock air and sea battle, with airplanes bombing with toilet paper, and ships shooting red dye and old Cuban bread.

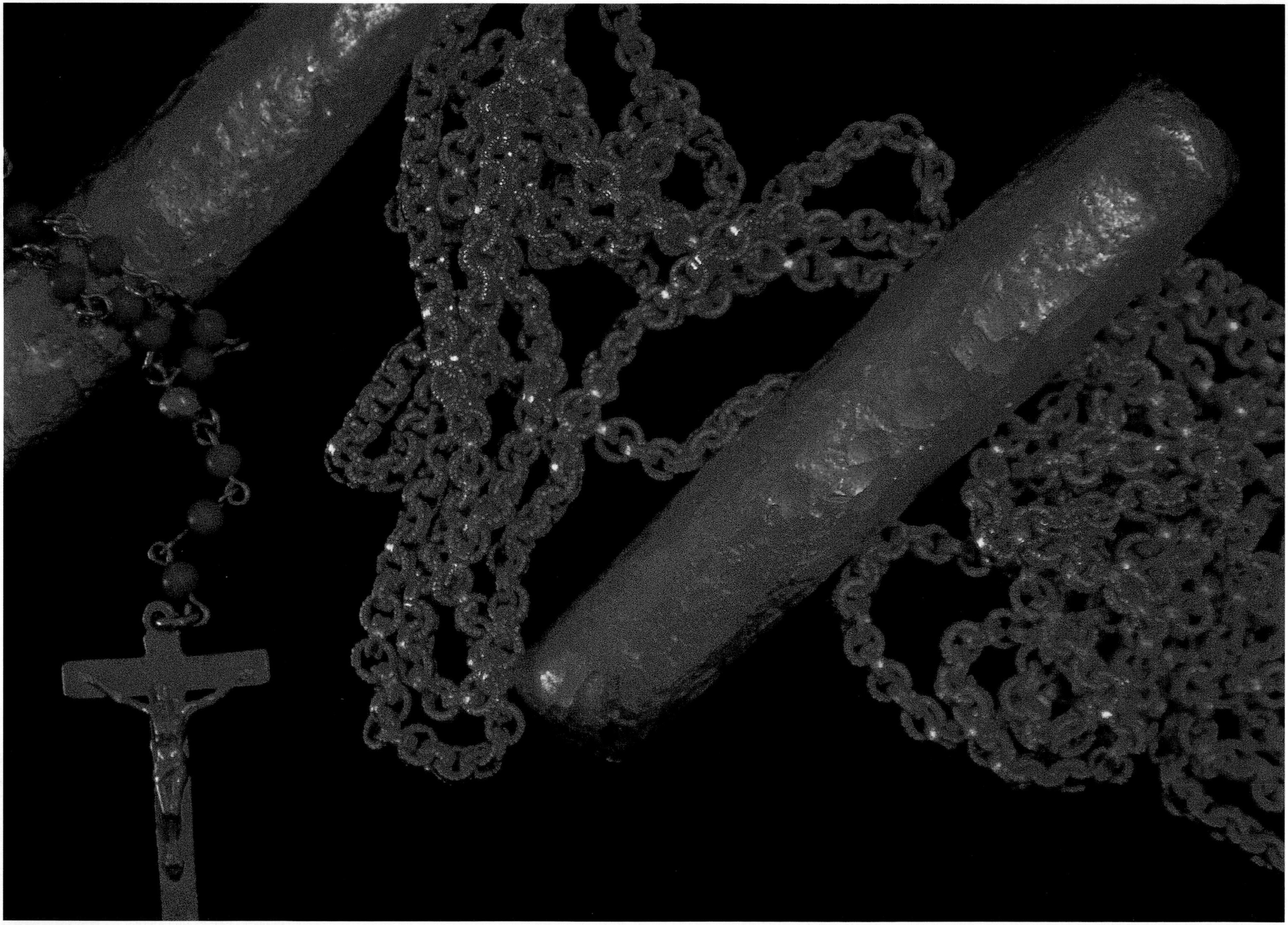

KEY WEST TREASURE CHEST   700 Front Street

On July 20, 1985, Mel Fisher, who is now acknowledged to be the world's greatest treasure hunter, received a marine radio transmission from his son, Kane, who was captain of one of the salvage vessels that had been searching for the Spanish galleon Atocha. Kanes's message was simple: "Put away the charts. We found the mother lode." Mel's life-long dream was about to be realized, because the "mother lode" in this case represented approximately $400,000,000 worth of gold, silver, emeralds and artifacts. After lying on the ocean floor for more than 360 years unmolested, the Atocha was finally giving up her riches. Thousands of gold and silver coins and bars, beautifully handcrafted gold link chains (some more than 50 feet in length), thousands of emeralds, and countless, priceless artifacts, including cannons, weapons, personal jewelry, ornate gold plates and goblets, and various types of pottery comprised the bounty. For 17 years, Mel's motto had been "Today's the day." July 20, 1985 actually became that day. Ironically, the discovery of this fortune came exactly ten years to the day after Mel and his devoted wife, Dolores, lost their son Dirk and daughter-in-law, Angel, when their salvage vessel, Northwind, took on water in the middle of the night and capsized, trapping the young couple and another diver, Rick Gage, inside the vessel.

In September of 1622, the Nuestra Senora de Atocha, along with 27 other ships of King Philip IV's Tierra Firme Fleet, left Havana, Cuba with Spain as their destination. Unfortunately, the vessels were caught in a severe hurricane, and eight ships, including the Atocha and the Santa Margarita, were destroyed by the treacherous reefs off the Florida Keys. The Atocha, as the flagship of the fleet, carried the most prominent passengers and widest assortment of treasures. Of its 265 passengers, only five individuals lived to tell the story.

In 1963, Mel had a fortuitous meeting with a Florida treasure hunter, Kip Wagner, who, along with his associates had been attempting to salvage the remains of the Spanish Fleet lost on the East Coast of Florida in 1715. Mel and Kip then became equal partners in their ventures. Although the 1715 Spanish shipwrecks were close to shore, and the divers were sometimes working in only ten feet of water, the water was extremely murky, and often visibility was zero. Fortunately, with Mel's engineering background he created a device he called a "mailbox" which, when lowered from the vessel would send a layer of clear water downward so that the divers could clearly see where they were working. The "mailbox" also was able to part the sand so that the divers could uncover the buried treasures. Over the next six years, the partners uncovered more than $20 million worth of treasures from the 1715 shipwrecks.

In 1968, Mel and his fledgling company, Treasure Salvors, Inc., began their search for one of the richest shipwrecks in history, the Nuestra Senora de Atocha. Over the next 17 years, Mel committed himself and his family to the quest of finding the Atocha, and he overcame personal, legal and financial trials that would have stopped anyone, except Mel Fisher.

In 1974, Mel sought the legal services of David Paul Horan. Over the next decade, Horan successfully litigated and defended Mel's companies, Treasure Salvors, Inc., and Cobb Coin Company, from claims of the United States of America, the State of Florida and numerous other opportunists. In 1982, Horan argued Fisher's case before the United States Supreme Court. In a 5 to 4 decision, the highest court in the land ruled that Treasure Salvors was the sole owner of everything recovered from the Nuestra Senora de Atocha. David Paul Horan, had become the world's foremost authority on the salvage of shipwrecks. Horan and his brother and law partner, Edward W. Horan, have been primary counsel for such notable shipwrecks as the RMS Titanic (lost in the North Atlantic in 1912), the SS Central America (lost off the East Coast of North America in 1857), the San Miguel de Archangel (lost off Florida's East Coast in 1659) and El Cazador (lost off Louisiana in 1784).

Judge William O. Mehrtens of the United States District Court of the Southern District of Florida summed up Mel's situation in his August 21, 1978 ruling against the State of Florida, when he stated: "The finding of a great treasure from the days of the Spanish Main is not the cherished dream of only the United States and Florida citizens; countless people from other lands have shared such thoughts. It would amaze and surprise most citizens of this country, when their dream, at the greatest of costs, was realized, that agents of respective governments would, on the most flimsy grounds, lay claim to the treasure."

The beautiful, exciting and authentic treasures of Key West Treasure Chest are, in part, the legal fees David Paul and Edward Horan received for their successful efforts regarding the Atocha, lost off the Florida Keys in 1622.

Photo of diver taken by Don Kincaid

AUDUBON HOUSE AND TROPICAL GARDENS
205 Whitehead Street

In the mid 1800s, Captain John Geiger, a wealthy wrecker, started to create this unique setting. John J. Audubon, the world-renowned naturalist, spent many days and nights as a guest of the captain and painted many of his celebrated birds of America in these surroundings. In 1960, Mitchell Wolfson, of Wometco fame, completed the restoration of this unique house and gardens. This oasis of lush plants and trees from around the world, coupled with dazzling displays of beautifully-colored flowers creates a respite of gentleness in Key West. Perhaps this is why so many brides and grooms choose this spot to pledge their love.

KEY WEST LIGHTHOUSE MUSEUM
938 Whitehead Street

The Key West Lighthouse was built in 1847. It replaced the original wooden tower on Whitehead Point, which was destroyed in the hurricane of 1846. The present location, 14 feet above sea level, was chosen to protect the new tower from a similar fate. This brick tower is 86 feet high; 88 steps inside lead to a balcony with a 360-degree view of Key West. This is one of the most attractive vantage points in Key West to view the entire island. In 1969, the U.S. Coastal Board decommissioned the Lighthouse. In 1989, it was restored as a historical site at a cost of $265,000.

The lighthouse keeper's quarters was built in 1887, and today houses the museum's collection of lighthouse artifacts and the maritime history of Key West.

PRESIDENTIAL GATES
Whitehead Street corner of Caroline

President Truman made these gates famous when he visited Key West. Each morning he began his five-mile constitutional walk through these gates, with secret service agents in tow. These beautiful gates were built in 1906, and until 1987 would only be opened for visiting dignitaries.

THE HARRY S. TRUMAN LITTLE WHITE HOUSE MUSEUM
111 Front Street

The Harry S. Truman Little White House Museum is a 8,700 square foot, two-story Victorian building which was constructed in 1890 at a cost of $7,000. In 1991 it was restored and opened as a museum at a cost of one million dollars. It was originally built as housing for the naval station commander. Thomas Edison lived here while donating his services to the U.S. World I effort in 1917.

This site has a history that dates back to 1823, when the U.S. Government eradicated the pirates of the area. It was also a strategic port for the Spanish-American War, a submarine base for World War II, and a much-discussed position during the Cuban Missile Crisis in 1962. Harry S. Truman, the 33rd President of the United States, first visited Key West in 1946. He liked the climate and enjoyed taking his five-mile morning constitutional walk. President Truman loved the fishing, and returned ten more times for a total of 175 days during his presidency, which lasted from 1945 to 1952.

After Truman paved the way, a number of other presidents utilized the attractive facilities of the Little White House. In 1955, President Eisenhower while recovering from a heart attack, held all his meetings in this house. In 1961, President Kennedy held a summit meeting here with Britain's Prime Minister three weeks before the Bay of Pigs Invasion, and just prior to the Vietnam buildup. A year later, immediately after the Cuban Missile Crisis, President Kennedy paid Key West another visit to assure the people of the United States it was safe to visit Florida.

THE CUSTOM HOUSE
AND

KEY WEST MUSEUM OF ART AND HISTORY
281 Front Street

This imposing 1891 magnificently designed redbrick building built in 1891, is a registered national landmark, and one of the most beautiful and important buildings in Key West. It cost approximately $110,000 to build. In 1999 a major restoration, which took nine years, was completed at a cost of nine million dollars. It originally served as a Federal Building, housing the Post Office and Custom Service. On the second floor was the Federal District Court, in which the original hearing was held to determine the cause of the sinking of the U.S.S. Maine in Havana in 1898.

Today the building serves as the Key West Museum of Art and History. There are ten to twelve exhibitions each year in addition to the permanent exhibits. "Who Is Key West" is a portrait collection of Key West notables and nefarious characters by nationally renowned artist Paul Collins. Because of its popularity, this exhibition is on extended loan from the artist.

This building is one of three historic buildings operated as museums by the Key West Art and Historical Society. The Key West Lighthouse and East Martello Tower (a Civil War Fort) are also operated by the society.

31

THE KEY WEST HISTORIC MEMORIAL GARDEN
Mallory Dock

The most compelling work of art in Key West today is "The Wreckers," the centerpiece of The Key West Historic Memorial Garden. This depicts two wreckers on a sinking ship with a little girl strapped to the back of one of the men. Her left arm is clinging to the neck of her savior and her right arm is holding her doll. Surrounding this emotional bronze is a series of 36 busts of the men and women who were important to the development of Key West, from 1821 until 1980. James Mastin, an award-winning sculptor from Miami, created "The Wreckers." Simonton, who purchased Key West in 1821, Flagler, who built the railroad, and Hemingway are all honored with their images cast in bronze, with plaques describing their importance to Key West.

This garden was created in September 1997 as a memorial to those courageous men and women who helped create the Key West we know today.

THE WRECKERS

KEY WEST CEMETERY
Center of Old Town
Bounded by Angela, Margaret,
Passover Lane , Frances, and Olivia

Where else in the world can one find a cemetery located in the heart of town, and spend an enjoyable half day reading tombstones, and chuckling or laughing out loud? In 1847 a severe hurricane washed away the entire graveyard and the dead were scattered throughout the forest, many of them lodged in the branches of nearby trees.

After that disaster, the cemetery was relocated to higher ground. Because of the rocky foundation of the island, all tombs are above ground. The largest and most visible gravesite is that of 27 sailors of the U.S.S. Maine, destroyed in Havana, Cuba in 1898. Although there was no concrete proof of responsibility for the act, the combination of the press and the outcry from the public forced the U.S. Government to declare war on Spain. Pictured below is a conch (born in Key West) woman who married in Key West, raised a family here, and now visits her husband who died a few years ago. She recently moved north, but whenever she returns, she visits her husband's grave site and enjoys a breakfast of a croissant and a cup of coffee.

On Violet Street you will find the grave of Joe Russell, proprietor of Sloppy Joe's, and a buddy and constant companion of Hemingway's. Russel died while deep-sea fishing with "Papa" in 1941. A number of blocks away, you will see the markings for Thomas Romer, a black Bohemian, with the inscription, "Good Citizen for 65 of his 108 years," signed by Gallagher, perhaps an opinionated stonecutter. Another grave has the inscription, "Devoted fan of Julio Iglesias." My favorite is the inscription on a crypt in the Jewish section of the cemetery that reads, "I told you I was sick." There is also an interesting comment, probably by a former wife, "At least I know where he is sleeping tonight."

KEY WEST AQUARIUM
1 Whitehead Street

In 1932, during the Great Depression, Key West was bankrupt. The Florida Emergency Relief Administration Fund was initiated by President Franklin Roosevelt to save the city. The Key West Aquarium was its first project, and was constructed from 1932 to 1934.

From the beginning, getting really close to the fish and animals has always been a unique part of the Aquarium's experience. The touch tank, which permits children and grown-ups to hold and touch the fish and animals, has always been a major attraction. The aquarium was renovated in 1983 and is now primarily enclosed. It has numerous tanks which house a large and beautiful collection of fish indigenous to the Keys. Shark feedings (eight times a day) have been thrilling crowds for decades.

KEY WEST BUTTERFLY AND NATURE CONSERVATORY
1316 Duval Street

Perhaps the most eye-catching and beautiful attraction in Key West is the 13,000 square foot Key West Butterfly and Nature Conservatory located at 1316 Duval Street. It is also Key West's newest attraction, having been completed in January 2003.

There are few attractions anywhere which appeal to young children, teenagers, their parents and grandparents. I have visited the conservatory four or five times, and have always been struck by the glee of the children and the wonderment in the eyes of the senior citizens. Virtually all visitors walk away from this butterfly world with a plastic butterfly attached to their shirt or sweater and a smile on their face.

The creators of this world of beauty are Sam Trophia and George Fernandez. They dreamed, planned and traveled the world to visit virtually every major conservatory. Their journey took them from Central, South, and North America, to Africa and Southeast Asia. Their aim was to build the best butterfly conservatory in the world. In addition to the 5,000 square foot glass-enclosed butterfly habitat are a learning center for children and a unique art gallery. There is also a beautifully decorated gift shop where it is extremely difficult to decide what to purchase because there are so many interesting, reasonably-priced choices available.

The partners' slogan is "Excite your senses, expand your mind." With over 60 varieties of butterflies, a few thousand plants, and at least 1,000 butterflies flying and landing on everything, that is exactly what happens. During one of my visits, two butterflies landed on my cap and stayed for a nice chat. . . The kids around me could not stop giggling and laughing at the sight!

CONCH TRAIN
Front Street

In 1959, Olive and Bill Kroll converted a dream into a money machine. With Olive selling tickets for $1.00 a ride, Bill would take the tourists on a ride, showing the prominent homes of Key West and other Key West attractions. In 1972, the large conglomerate, Wometco, purchased the Kroll's dream and in 1983 it was resold to Historic Tours of America.

The rides are open 365 days a year and utilize 14 trains (the cars are converted jeeps) which can comfortably accommodate 56 passengers. With inflation, the cost of today's ride has increased slightly to $20.00 per head. Over 11 million passengers have enjoyed the conch train ride over the past 44 years.

SOUTHERNMOST POINT
Ocean and Whitehead Street

There are more "Kodak moments" shot at the Southernmost Point of the United States than at any home, attraction, or sunset in Key West. Virtually every person visiting paradise finds his or her way to this fascinating spot. For at least 70 years, there has been a monument or sign designating this area and proclaiming "Cuba 90 Miles." The current monument dates to 1983.

For over 50 years, the Kee Clan, originally from China, has been selling conch shells to tourists who come to have their picture taken at the Southernmost Point. Originally "Yankee" and his brother "Chinaman" started the business. Yankee's son, Albert, carried on in his father's footsteps.

MALLORY SQUARE

Because of its daily sunset festivals, which begin two hours before sunset, Mallory Square is one of the most famous locations in Key West. In the mid–1800s, the Mallory docks, then a series of wooden decks, catered to the wrecking business. That industry pushed Key West into the limelight and helped it become the richest city per capita in the United States. In 1963, the old wooden planks were exchanged for a concrete base, and in 1990 the piers were revamped for cruise ship use.

Every night there is a gathering of thousands, mostly tourists, who come to watch the ever-changing performance of skilled entertainers, and mingle with fifty or so artisans selling their hand-crafted jewelry, photos, clothing and numerous other items. However, this is all a preamble, because once the setting sun begins to flirt with the horizon, all attention is galvanized toward the water and the setting sun's gentle surrender to the horizon.

FORT ZACHARY TAYLOR
Historic State Park and Public Beach

This beautiful 87 acre park, with attractively curved beaches, is a national landmark that has played a significant roll in Florida's early development. Construction on the fort began in 1845 and continued until 1866. The fort was never completed. The fort has a very strategic location overlooking the Atlantic Ocean, and Gulf of Mexico. In 1850, it was named after President Zachary Taylor, who had died earlier that year.

In 1861, when the Civil War began, Captain John Brannon and his men occupied the fort on behalf of the Union Army. President Lincoln had ordered a blockade of all Southern ports. Fort Taylor made Key West an effective port to operate because their cannons had a three-mile range. During the Civil War, 199 confederate ships were captured trying to run the blockade. The fort was also used in the Spanish-American War, and World War I and II. The fort currently has the largest collection of Civil War artifacts in America.

When Fort Taylor was opened as a state park, its 1,000-foot beach was a wonderful addition to the limited beaches in Key West. Although the beaches are lovely, I would suggest having some footwear when you go swimming at Fort Taylor because of the numerous rocks in the water. The West Side of the park is ideal for fishing. There are picnic tables, showers, and a concession stand.

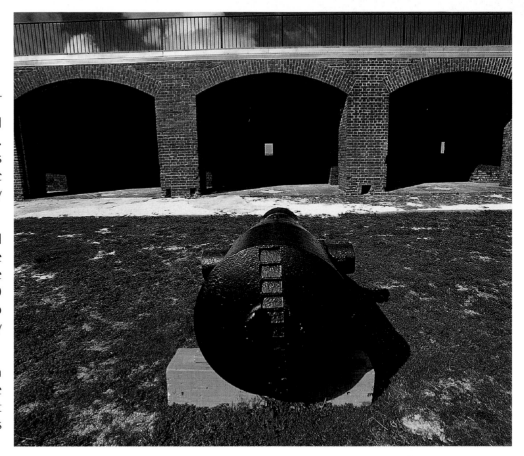

SMATHERS BEACH
South Roosevelt Boulevard

One mile from the Key West Airport, along the Atlantic Ocean, is Smathers Beach, named for Senator George Smathers. In 1961, the Senator was instrumental in getting federal funding, which helped create this beach. Smathers Beach runs for approximately one half mile in length, with numerous volleyball courts, rest facilities, and food vendors. This beach is a favorite with the tourists.

CLARENCE S. HIGGS MEMORIAL BEACH
South Roosevelt Boulevard

Higgs Beach was originally christened Monroe County Beach in April, 1949. Shortly thereafter, County Commissioner Higgs died and the name of the beach was changed in his honor. This manmade beach, jutting into the Atlantic slightly south of Smathers Beach, has a retaining wall, and a fascinating pier, with cleverly painted footsteps. The beach is adjacent to an old Civil War fort named West Martello Tower. Higgs Beach is a popular beach with the residents of Key West.

SHELL WAREHOUSE
1 Whitehead Street

If you love beachcombing and shell collecting as I do, the Shell Warehouse is a wonderful spot to enjoy and pick up a few small trinkets.

SUNSET KEY

In 1994, the property formally known as Tank Island was sold. This beautiful 27-acre property, a three-minute boat ride from Key West, has now been transformed into a tropical Island of elegance, beauty, and charm. The beaches are pristine and reminiscent of the silky, soft, white sands of the Caribbean. Millions of dollars have been invested into this unique vision. The natural beauty of this location combined with the creative and talented professional builders of Sunset Key has already attracted many families looking for their tropical paradise.

CRUISE LINES

The cruise ship industry is the fastest growing segment of the tourist trade in Key West. In 2003 approximately 1,000,000 passengers walked the planks into the golden sunshine of Key West. During the previous four years, that number had been under 700,000 travelers with small increases each year. In 1990, approximately 100,000 individuals disembarked in Key West to walk Duval Street for a number of hours, and in 1995 that had already increased to approximately 375,000 tourists, seeking a conch train ride or a beer at Sloppy Joe's.

Back in the mid-1970s, it was Carnival Cruise Line that pioneered the way with a new concept. The "Fun Cruise" was born, with flashy ships, great entertainment and gaudy casinos. This appealed to a mass market of young, first-time cruisers from all walks of life. The concept was brilliant! Today Carnival Corporation is the largest cruise ship company in the world, owning Carnival, Holland American, Cunard, Seabourn, Windstar and Costa Cruise Lines, with sales of approximately 4 billion dollars a year.

Opposite page-Carnival Glory

FLAT FISHING – DEEP-SEA FISHING

Tens of thousands of anglers come to Key West every year to fish. Dedicated golfers go to Scotland, and dedicated flat and sport fishermen come to paradise.

Norman Woods, Sr. is considered to be the father of Key West Marlin fishing. For many years it was well known that marlins were off the coast of Key West, as Hemingway proved in his years of fishing between Key West and Cuba. Beginning in the mid-1970s, Woods and his fishing buddy, Wayne Hunt, began searching for the escarpment, which drops 800 feet. The escarpment, or wall, runs parallel to the entire East Coast, and curves around the Keys and the Dry Tortugas and up into the Gulf of Mexico. This ridge creates an upwelling of nutrients on which baitfish feed. Larger fish feed on the baitfish, and the food chain continues as larger game fish feed on the other fish. One historic day in 1981 Woods found his paradise; he had seven marlins hooked and landed four of them. "We knew there had to be a drop off somewhere, and when we researched the charts we figured out where it had to be." The part of the escarpment of the lower keys is now known as "Woods' Wall," in honor of the pioneer who discovered it.

There are three members of the marlin family: the White Marlin, the Striped Marlin, and the big daddy, the Blue Marlin. They can range from 100 to 1,100 pounds and depending on the fish, the fisherman, the crew, and captain of the boat, the battle to catch the marlin can take from ten minutes to many hours.

61

FUN IN THE SUN

Before the sun sneaks away for a little nap and the serious partying begins, Key West is a camp for grown-ups with few restrictions and no counselors. There seems to be at least 15 varieties of automated transportation, including three-wheeled cars, electric cars, electric eggs, etc., which all seem to be carefree and fun, but certainly not inexpensive. Fishing, snorkeling, sailing, and scuba diving lure a high percentage of tourists. But don't forget wave running, kayaking, wind surfing, sunfish sailing, water skiing, speed boating, parasailing, jet skiing, roller blading, skateboarding, and that old time sport . . . swimming.

Opposite page: The beautiful catamaran, Stars & Stripes - Captained by Don Kincaid

THE DRY TORTUGAS – FORT JEFFERSON

The most exciting adventure I experienced in Key West was a four-hour trip to the Dry Tortugas with Seaplanes of Key West. This national park lies in the blue-green waters of the Gulf of Mexico, 70 miles due west of Key West. The 40-minute plane ride is thrilling. Usually, the seaplane flies at an altitude of only 500 feet and the shallow waters enable you to see numerous shipwrecks lying in beautiful sparkling waters. If you are lucky, you may also get to see stingrays, porpoises, or sharks.

The Spanish explorer, Ponce De Leon discovered the islands in 1513. He named these seven small islands, La Tortugas (The Turtles), due to the abundance of sea turtles. The word "dry" was later added to mariners' charts to warn of the lack of fresh water. The first construction in 1825 on Garden Key, the largest of the seven islands, was a lighthouse to warn sailors of rocky shoals. Construction of Fort Jefferson began in 1846. The United States Military knew it could control the navigation to the Gulf of Mexico and protect Atlantic-bound trade by fortifying the Tortugas. For over 30 years, and utilizing over 16,000,000 bricks, construction continued on the 11 acres on Garden Key. However, the fort was never completed.

Continued on page 67

THE DRY TORTUGAS *continued*

During the Civil War, the fort was used by the north as a military prison for captured deserters. It also held Dr. Samuel Mudd, who was convicted of complicity in the assassination of President Lincoln in 1865. Because of the heroic work Dr. Mudd did during a yellow fever epidemic at the fort, which saved both soldiers and prisoners, he was pardoned, but not exonerated by President Jackson. Today a number of relatives of Dr. Mudd are still fighting in court to have him exonerated. However, there seems to be little doubt that he was involved in a conspiracy to kidnap Lincoln, lead by John Wilkes Booth, and therefore it is unlikely his relatives will be successful.

The invention of the rifled cannon made the fort obsolete because its thick walls could be penetrated. The army abandoned Fort Jefferson in 1874. In 1935 the fort was proclaimed a national monument, and in 1992, the Dry Tortugas reached its current status as a national park.

The Dry Tortugas are also a marine wilderness, and the main island is partially surrounded by beautiful beaches, which encourage snorkeling enthusiasts. Most of the individuals reach the island via catamarans and various schooners, which are housed in Key West.

DUVAL STREET
Day

Duval Street begins at the Gulf of Mexico and runs for almost two miles with the Atlantic Ocean its final destination. Between these two beautiful bodies of water lie fourteen blocks of numerous restaurants, guesthouses, many excursion booths, hundreds of retail stores, and at least 436 T-shirt shops. During the day, these streets are the spokes of the wheel of Key West, as they teem with sightseers, shoppers, gays, straights, men, and women of all ages who have been lured by the hype of the southernmost city in the United States.

DUVAL STREET
Night

Key West comes alive at night, orchestrated by bars like Sloppy Joe's, Hog's Breath, Captain Tony's, and numerous others, which are directly on Duval or just a few steps away. Most bars have singers and bands to compete for the business of the tourists who have come to Key West to laugh, drink, and drink some more. At 1 a.m. most nights, there are generally more people walking the heart of Duval, than at 1 p.m., many with beer cans and bottles, and a little more boisterous than they were a few hours before. Duval at night is reminiscent of the French Quarter of New Orleans.

SLOPPY JOE'S
201 Duval Street

To me, Sloppy Joe's is the most famous bar in the world, with Rick's of Casablanca fame a close second. Back in the early 1930s, it was christened "Hemingway's Bar" by the Key West Chamber of Commerce. At that time, Sloppy Joe's was operating 24 hours a day; gin sold for 10 cents a shot, and a tall cool glass of beer, cost a nickle.

The original Sloppy Joe's, also world renowned, was located 90 miles southwest in Havana, Cuba. In 1928, when Hemingway first visited Key West, Joe Russell (Sloppy Joe), had already opened his gin mill, and was also captain of his own fishing boat. Joe Russell almost immediately became a key player in what was described as the Hemingway Mob, which included writer John Dos Passos.

Russell moved Sloppy Joe's three times. In mid-1937, at the expiration of his lease and after a disagreement with his landlord, he gave Key West something to talk about. At the stroke of midnight, he gathered all his drinking buddies together and literally ripped out the bar, the mirror, the fixtures, (including the urinals), and moved them to an empty location down the street. Joe paid off his moving men with free beers, and the drinking continued into the wee hours of the morning. Hemingway himself ended up with one of the urinals, which is currently on display in the garden of the Ernest Hemingway Home and Museum. In future years, Hemingway's comment concerning the Sloppy Joe's midnight move was, "Only in Key West."

THE CURRY MANSION INN
511 Caroline Street

William Curry was a penniless Bahamian when he first arrived in Key West in the 1820s. He later became the Treasurer of Key West, and was also credited with operating an unofficial bank for businesses and individuals. He is generally considered to be the first millionaire in Key West. Salvaging goods from the hapless ships which were engulfed by the coral reefs helped create his fortune. In the early years, many of the inhabitants of Key West considered the pirates and the scavengers of salvage as two peas in a pod.

Curry started building his mansion in 1867. Curry, like all wreckers who built homes in Key West, incorporated architectural details from many ports of call such as balustrades from New Orleans, columns from the deep South and the widow walks from New England. In 1905, the younger Curry constructed a new house on the original plot.

The 11,000 square foot house is furnished with 18th Century antiques and Victorian pieces, creating a charming and interesting throwback to a bygone era.

THE SOUTHERNMOST HOUSE
1400 Duval Street

This magnificent example of Queen Ann architecture is the shinning jewel of Key West. Judge J. Vinning Harris built this elegant structure in the early 1900s. Mrs. Harris, formerly Florida Curry, was the daughter of William Curry.

During the 1940s, this home was converted into a popular waterfront restaurant and gambling club, known as the Casa Cayo Hueso Club. It attracted many notables, such as Walter P. Chrysler and Tennessee Williams. The house became a private residence again after being purchased by Hilario and Placeres

Ramos. Their children Charles and Mathilde, are the current owners. Charles Ramos has the distinction of being elected to the State Legislature in 1961 when he was only 24 years of age. Mr. Ramos also served as City Commissioner of Key West.

The Southernmost House has recently become a historic museum, with numerous, fascinating one-of-a-kind photos and documents of the history of Key West. This unique guest house, which is privileged by having it's own private beach, plays host to numerous romantic weddings using the Atlantic Ocean as a backdrop. There is also a beautiful outside bar area, surrounded by an inviting pool, which is attractively landscaped with potted plants and trees. This gorgeous oasis seems to have it all!

THE OCTAGON HOUSE
712 Eaton

The house at 712 Eaton has the unusual distinction of answering to three names. The Richard Peacon Jr. House, The Octagon House, and the Calvin Klein House.

Merchant Richard Peacon Jr., originally from the Bahamas, was the owner of Key West's largest grocery store. He completed 712 Eaton in 1899. Overflowing palms create a warm and inviting atmosphere surrounding this shimmering white house, adding to its romantic architectural lines. One of its nicknames, the Octagon House, is derived from its unusual facade, which is unique in Key West. Its elegance, both inside and out, has attracted two famous designers. In 1974, Angela Donghia purchased the house for $45,000 from Mrs. Chester Curry, the daughter of Richard Peacon. In 1980, after being renovated and restored by Fred Cole, the house was sold to Calvin Klein for $975,000, which up until that date was the highest price ever paid for a home in Key West. In less than a year, Klein lost his lust for Key West, and resold the house at a substantial loss. This only proves "Paradise" is not for everyone.

THE GINGERBREAD HOUSE
615 Elizabeth Street

It is beautiful. . . It is unique. . . without a doubt, the best example of a large conch house with elaborate gingerbread details on the island. In 1870, Benjamin Baker, a Bahamian by birth, built the original structure, which over the years has undergone substantial renovation. Mr. Baker was a prominent citizen of Key West, serving as City Commissioner, as well as owning numerous businesses, which included undertaking, wrecking, sponging, and retail stores. Some of the old-timers of Key West, refer to this house as "The Wedding Cake House."

In 1885 the house was transferred to Mr. Baker's daughter when she married a gentlemen by the name of Illingsworth. The house stayed in the Baker-Illingsworth family for over 100 years, until it was sold in 1972. In 1995, this house was the recipient of the Preservation Award.

THE ERNEST HEMINGWAY HOUSE AND MUSEUM

907 Whitehead

The Man

The Hemingway myth is alive and flourishing in Key West. Even now, forty years after his death, the man who branded himself "Papa" while in his thirties, has continued to consume Key West and many of its tourists. The Hemingway saga, his writings, photos, articles and stories (including fabricated tall tales), live on in Key West through the Hemingway House, Sloppy Joe's, and numerous other retail establishments (who know that Hemingway paraphernalia sells. . . and sells big!).

Ernest and his second wife Pauline arrived in Key West in 1928. Hemingway was 28 years of age and a relatively unknown writer. When he left twelve years later in 1940, he had already published most of his important works and was world renowned for both his writing and the mystique which surrounded him.

The House

The Hemingway Estate is a one-acre, beautifully landscaped palatial home, guarded by a five-foot brick wall, which surrounds the property. Asa F. Tift, a successful merchant and shipbuilder originally built the house in 1851. Many conchs still refer to this house as the Asa Tift House. The house is constructed of limestone blocks from Key West, and was later remodeled. At the height of the depression in 1931, the Tift House was in deplorable condition and was in foreclosure. Gus Pfeiffer, Pauline's uncle, purchased the house from the bank for $8,000 and gave it to the Hemingways. A catwalk was built from the second level of Hemingway's writing studio to make it

continued next page

easier for him to go back and forth from the main house to his studio. In 1938, while Papa was covering the war in Spain, Pauline, in a futile attempt to save her marriage and to keep Hemingway away from the beautiful, bright, sexy writer, Martha Gellhorn, built a large swimming pool in their backyard. This was the very first pool in Key West. When he returned from Spain, in typical Hemingway fashion, he proclaimed to Pauline and to all his friends that the pool had cost him his last penny, as he tossed a penny on the ground and stated, "You might as well take my last cent." Pauline had that penny permanently fixed in cement at the edge of the pool where it remains today. It's interesting to note Pauline, not Hemingway, paid for the pool.

SIMONTON COURT HISTORIC INN & COTTAGES
320 Simonton Street

The combination of archways built with thousands of tiny magenta bougainvillea leaves, coupled with radiant flowers from orchid trees, create a setting in this garden that could lead to the Gates of Heaven. Strangely enough, the inn of this little paradise was a cigar factory in the 1870s, where tobacco leaves were dried, rolled and stored. Across from the inn is a series of small cottages, whose original tenants were the workers of the cigar factory. Today these cottages are surrounded by an impressive collection of palms, banana trees, ficus hedges, gardenia plants, orchids and bougainvillea which create an exotic atmosphere.

ST. PAUL'S EPISCOPAL CHURCH
401 Duval Street

Since 1832, St. Paul's has had a strong influence on Key West. In those days the real estate tax was set at "not more than one half of one percent," and unimproved land, which was almost the entire island, was valued at $25.00 per acre. In December 1832, John William Charles Fleming, who was one of the founding fathers of Key West, was buried on church ground. The church now stands on land given to St. Paul's by Mrs. J.W.C. Fleming for a consideration of $1.00.

The church has proved its resiliency by living through three major fires and three serious hurricanes. The church was destroyed on numerous occasions. The magnificent white masonry church currently on display with its beautiful stained-glass windows was built in 1919. The beautiful tree in full bloom in front of the church is a Royal Poinciana. It bursts into bloom just before the rainy season and blossoms like a flame. Its scarlet blooms are shed about two months later when the tree leafs out. The churchyard has a myriad of plants that grow in the tropics. The crotons, ixora and other plants from Africa add color to the landscape of the garden, which also houses numerous palms, West Indian mahoganies, and various other small plants and ferns.

In back of the church is a small cemetery. There are major plans to change the landscape with waterfalls, an altar, and additional new plants. Although the gardens are beautiful, the new plans seem very exciting.

JOE ALLEN GARDEN CENTER
WEST MORTELLO TOWER
White Street at the Atlantic Ocean

I remember vividly my first visit to the Joe Allen Garden Center, which is cloistered in the West Mortello Tower. There was a major rainstorm and the huge drops felt like soggy pellets as they were attacking me. The plants and trees were glistening from the rain, appearing as if they had received three coats of shellac.

The West Mortello Tower is all that remains of a fort that was used in the Civil War. Years later, this fort was used for target practice for the large guns at Fort Taylor. Understandably, the entire remains were extremely unattractive and it was scheduled for demolition by the city of Key West. In 1949, a group of prisoners from the local jail arrived with sledgehammers to level the remains of the fort. Fate stepped in with the passing by of State Representative Joe Allen, who halted the destruction and shortly thereafter started to create a beautiful tropical garden, which became the Joe Allen Garden Center.

Since 1955, the Key West Garden Club has had the responsibility to care for, nurture, and enhance the Joe Allen Garden Center. There are 200 members of the garden club which meets once a month. Many of the members' personal gardens are the starting points for numerous plants before they are transplanted to the Joe Allen Garden Center.

NANCY FORRESTER'S SECRET GARDEN
Free School Lane

Discretely hidden off Simmonton, in the center of Old Town, is this unique acre of land consumed with trees, plants, and numerous parrots, which help create the feeling of a bygone era. When Charles Kuralt visited Nancy in her Secret Garden, he was thrilled to find her unusual collection of palms and flowers, which includes over a hundred varieties of palms from all over the world. This unusual collection has been brought together by Nancy and her many helpers for the past 30 years. One of her recent co-creators of the garden is Norman Aberle, an artist himself, and also the Curator of the Key West Museum of Art and History at the Custom House. After 20 years of creating a special habitat, Nancy opened her garden to the public in December 1994, with the following statement. "With every square inch of the island being covered with concrete, I needed to nurture myself with a garden, to stay in tune with the earth . . . I hope that people will come here and use it as a respite from the asphalt jungle. It's cool and tranquil and soothing here. It nourishes my spirit and soul."

Nancy's 17 parrots have begun to encroach on the time she can spend on the garden. Recently, when we met with Nancy, the general topic of conversation centered around her beautiful parrots. My associate took the time to teach Ara, a female macaw (opposite page), how to lift one of her wings. Nancy was very pleased with the new trick. Unfortunately, we didn't have enough time to spend with Dulce, a male Umbrella Cockatoo, who is pictured below.

SUNSET KEY

The most unique and beautiful dining experience in a Key West vacation begins with a delightful (free) three-minute boat ride to the Island of Sunset Key. You will immediately be transported into a world of gentle breezes and elegant service, while dining on or near the beach, at the Lattitudes Restaurant. This romantic setting sets the mood for artistically-prepared delicious cuisine, while you await the sunset.

A few months ago while we were enjoying our dinner, we noticed a young, adorable couple sitting nearby. When the young lady excused herself, the young man leaned over and told us he was very nervous because he was going to propose after dinner, down at the dock. Fortunately, I had my camera and a short time later, although I was 300 yards away, I documented this romantic scene.